The Vocabulary of

SHOPPING

Downtown and Around Town

Raymond C. Clark

Illustrations by Nancy Shrewsbury Nadel

with photographs by the author

Pro Lingua Associates, Publishers
74 Cotton Mill Hill, Suite A315
Brattleboro, Vermont 05302 USA
Office: 802-257-7779
Orders: 800-366- 4775
Email: info@ProLinguaAssociates.com
WebStore: www.ProLinguaAssociates.com
SAN: 216-0579

At Pro Lingua
our objective is to foster an approach
to learning and teaching that we call
***interplay**, the **inter**action of language*
learners and teachers with their materials,
with the language and culture,
and with each other in active, creative,
*and productive **play**.*

Copyright © 2020 Raymond C. Clark

ISBN 978-0-86647-500-6; CD ISBN 978-0-86647-501-3; text/CD set ISBN 978-0-86647-502-0

This book was designed and set by Arthur A. Burrows using the sans-serif typeface Candara, developed in 2005 for Microsoft by Gary Munch and published by Ascender. Sans-serif faces often appear to be stiff and mechanical, and though easy to read in short texts, they lack grace. This face, designed for digital reading, is said to be friendly, playful, and humanist. The letter shapes are open; the lines subtly flared. It is elegant when used for display or in small phrases, and comfortable to read in extended text.

The photographs are by the author and from Dreamstime.com Agency: front cover image © Bymandesigns, title page © Madrabothair. The pen and ink drawings throughout are by Nancy Shrewsbury Nadel.

The book was printed and bound by McNaughton & Gunn in Saline, Michigan.

Printed in the United States of America
First edition 2020

CONTENTS

Learner's Guide
How to Use This Book

This book is about the words we use when we go shopping. There are 11 units. Each unit is about a place where we shop. In each unit there are 15-20 key words and 10 activities using these words. You may know some of them, but there are other words in the unit that you may not know. With this book you can increase your vocabulary by about 250 words. You can also improve your language skills (speaking, listening, reading, writing) and practice your grammar skill. Follow these steps as you go through a unit.

1. The first page has photos of the shopping place. You and your classmates can begin the unit by talking about these places -- How often do you go there? What is your favorite place? What do you do there? Also on the first page there are key words. With a friend or small group, find words you know and do not know. Share your knowledge.

2. The second page is a reading. First, try to read and understand it yourself. Then check your understanding with the questions on the next page.

3. The third activity (ANSWER) checks your understanding of the reading. First say the answers to yourself. Then say them to a partner. Next, you can write the answers and have your teacher check them, or go to the Pro Lingua website for the free answer booklet. (www.ProLinguaAssociates.com). Finally, read the second page reading again while listening to the audio to check the pronunciation of the words in the reading.

4. The fourth activity is a listening activity in which a person at the shopping place talks about the place. There is an audio CD available to use, or your teacher can speak this part. First, do not look at the page as you listen. Then talk about what you heard. Next, listen and follow along with the reading. Discuss again. Then listen again without looking.

5. The fifth activity is a kind of quiz to see how you are doing. Check your answers with a classmate or your teacher, or go to the website.

6. This activity is a back-and-forth activity to do with a classmate for speaking and listening practice. Take turns doing both parts of the exchange.

7. In this activity listen to the conversation. If you have the audio CD, play it first. If not, you can read it with a classmate. Do it at least four times; then try to do the conversation by looking at only the first two words, looking up and saying the entire line. Finally you can say it to another pair or the whole class.

8. In this TELL AND WRITE activity, you will review the conversation, but write about it as something that happened in the past. Check you answers with your teacher or the website.

9. This activity asks you to be creative and apply what you have practiced.

10. This final activity asks you to go to one of the places and do some simple research. Be sure the people at the place know why you are doing this. Bring your unit or the book to show them.

You can also use this book for self-study. To do this we suggest that you download or print out the answers from our website: www.ProLinguaAssociates.com. It will also be good to use the audio CD.

The Supermarket

an entrance	a department	frozen food	closed
an exit	produce	meat	express
a shopping basket	dairy	an aisle	a cashier
a shopping bag	bakery	a checkout	an employee
a shopping cart	deli	seafood	open

READ

This supermarket has

    7 departments.

They are:

    produce
    deli
    dairy
    bakery
    seafood
    meat
    frozen food

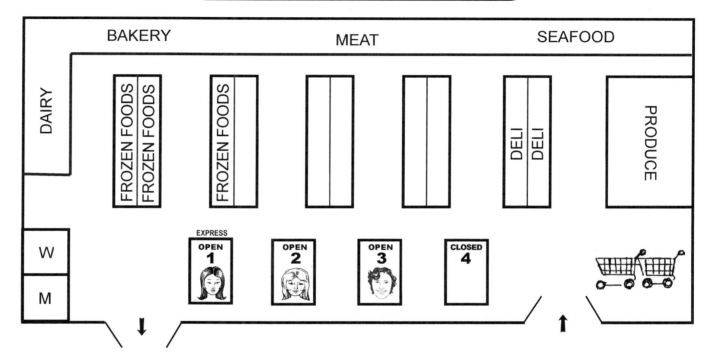

There are 6 aisles.

There are 4 checkouts.

    Checkouts 1, 2, and 3 are open.

    Checkout 4 is closed.

    Checkout 1 is express.

There are 3 cashiers. The cashiers are employees.

There are many employees at the supermarket.

ANSWER

1. How many departments are there? _____

2. How many aisles are there? _____

3. How many checkouts are there? _____

4. How many checkouts are open? _____

5. How many checkouts are closed? _____

6. How many checkouts are express? _____

7. How many cashiers are there? _____

8. How many employees are there? _____

LISTEN

Hi. I'm Chuck.

Welcome to my supermarket.

I am the manager.

This is the entrance.

Enter here and take a cart.

Put your shopping bags in the cart.

The produce department and deli are on the right.

The seafood and meat departments are in the back.

The bakery is in the back left corner.

The dairy department is on the left.

The frozen food department is also on the left.

ANSWER

manager	entrance	enter	take
cart	bags	produce	put
bakery	seafood	frozen	
dairy	right	side	

1. The _____ foods department is on the left.

2. This is the entrance. You _____ here.

3. Chuck is the _____ .

4. The _____ and _____ departments are in the left corner.

5. Get a shopping _____ at the _____ .

6. _____ your shopping _____ in the cart.

7. The _____ department is in the _____ corner.

8. Enter here and _____ a cart.

9. The _____ department is on the right _____.

ASK AND ANSWER

 Jeff

 Jane

How much is/are _____? It is/They are _____ .

Where can I find _____? It is/They are in the _____ department.

○ sweet potatoes $.69/ lb	○ ground beef $3.99/ lb	○ butter $2.99/ lb	○ large raw shrimp $9.99/ lb
○ frozen berries $7.99 3lb pkg	○ chocolate cake $9.99 ea	○ sliced bologna $4.99/ 3 oz.	○ fresh strawberries 2 1lb pkgs $5.00
○ chicken breast $1.99/ lb	○ fresh catfish $4.99/ lb	○ ricotta cheese $3.19/ 32 oz	○ large supreme pizza $7.69 ea
○ crab cake $1.00 ea / 2.5 oz	○ plain yoghurt $1.38/ 5.4 oz	○ bagels $2.29/ 4-pk	○ German potato salad $3.59 pkg
○ pork chops $1.79/ lb	○ tabouli salad $4.99/ 14 oz	○ delicious apples $ .89/ lb	○ chocolate chip cookies $2.99/ 5oz pkg

LISTEN AND SAY

Bev

Hugh

Do you have the shopping bags?
You take the cart.

Of course. We have four.
OK. Let's go.

Do you have the shopping list?
No, I don't. But I know what we need.
Yes. We need lettuce and potatoes.

No, I don't. Do you have it?
Do we need vegetables?
OK. . . . . . Here's the bakery.

We need a loaf of bread.

For dinner, meat or seafood?

Let's get seafood.

What about milk?

No. We don't need milk.

Let's get some ice cream.

Right! Frozen food is in aisle 6.

So, is that all?

That's it!

How many items?

Five.

Let's go to checkout one.
It's the express lane.

TELL AND WRITE

What did they do?

took	cart	*They took* _____
had	shopping bags	_____
didn't have	list	_____
knew	needed	_____
needed	potatoes	_____
got	seafood	_____
didn't need	milk	_____
got	ice cream	_____

WRITE AND DO

Make a shopping list and then go to a supermarket with a friend. Find the aisle for each food.

Shopping List

NEED	AISLE	NEED	AISLE
_____	_____	_____	_____
_____	_____	_____	_____
_____	_____	_____	_____
_____	_____	_____	_____
_____	_____	_____	_____
_____	_____	_____	_____
_____	_____	_____	_____

LOOK AROUND AND DO IT

Go to a supermarket and make a map showing the entrance, the exit, departments, aisles, checkouts, customer service.

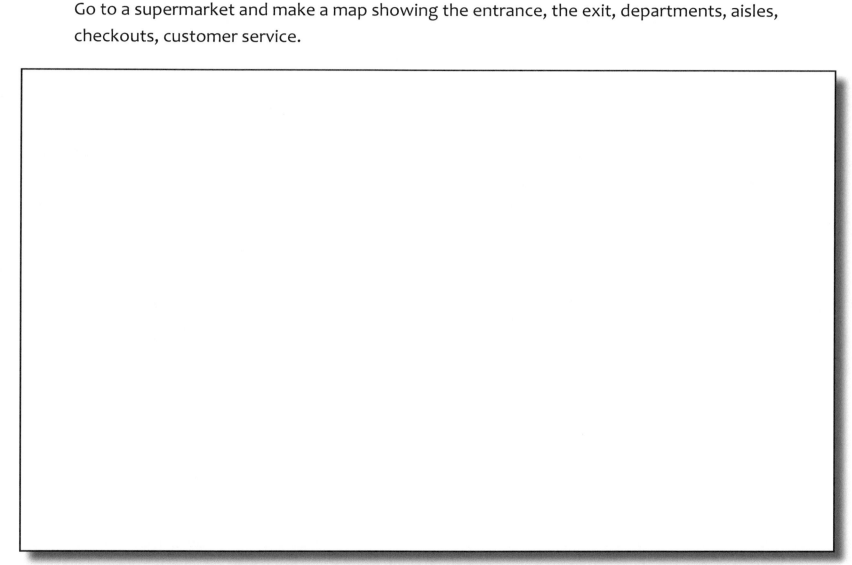

Note: It is advisable to explain to the department managers why you are doing this.

The Meat and Seafood Departments

MEAT	
beef	chicken
pork	ground beef
lamb	sausage
poultry	hot dogs

SEAFOOD		
shellfish	crabs	catfish
clams	shrimp	tilapia
mussels	calamari	flounder
scallops	salmon	cod

READ

We are at the meat and seafood departments.

The meat department is beside the seafood department.

In the meat department there are many packages of meat.

There is beef, pork, lamb, and poultry.

We make hamburgers with ground beef.

One kind of sausage is hot dogs.

One kind of poultry is chicken.

There are many kinds of seafood in the seafood department.

There are clams, mussels, and scallops. They are shellfish.

There are crabs, shrimp, and calamari.

There are many kinds of fish. Salmon, cod, catfish, tuna, and tilapia are fish.

ANSWER

1. Where is the meat department? _____

2. Where is the ground beef? _____

3. Where is the salmon? _____

4. What are clams and scallops? _____

5. What are cod, catfish, tuna, and tilapia? _____

6. What are salmon, shrimp, and scallops? _____

7. What do we make with ground beef? _____

8. How many packages of meat are there? _____

9. How many kinds of seafood are there? _____

10. What are hot dogs? _____

11. What is chicken? _____

LISTEN

My name is Jean.

I manage the seafood department.

We have fresh and frozen seafood.

Some seafood is wild-caught.

Some seafood is farm-raised.

My name is Jon.

I am the manager of the meat department.

I have many kinds of meat.

There are beefsteaks.

They are red meat.

There is also lamb and pork.

Chickens, ducks, and turkeys are poultry.

Chicken breast is white meat,

but thighs, wings, and legs are dark meat.

ANSWER

manages	breast	wild-caught	pork
red	poultry	frozen	fresh
seafood	dark		

1. Fresh fish are not _____.

2. Farm-raised fish are not _____ .

3. Jon _____ the meat department.

4. Jean manages the _____ department.

5. Chickens, ducks, and geese are _____.

6. Beef is _____ meat.

7. Chicken _____ is white meat.

8. Chicken thighs are _____ meat.

9. Lamb and _____ are meats.

10. There is both _____ and frozen fish in the seafood department

ASK AND ANSWER

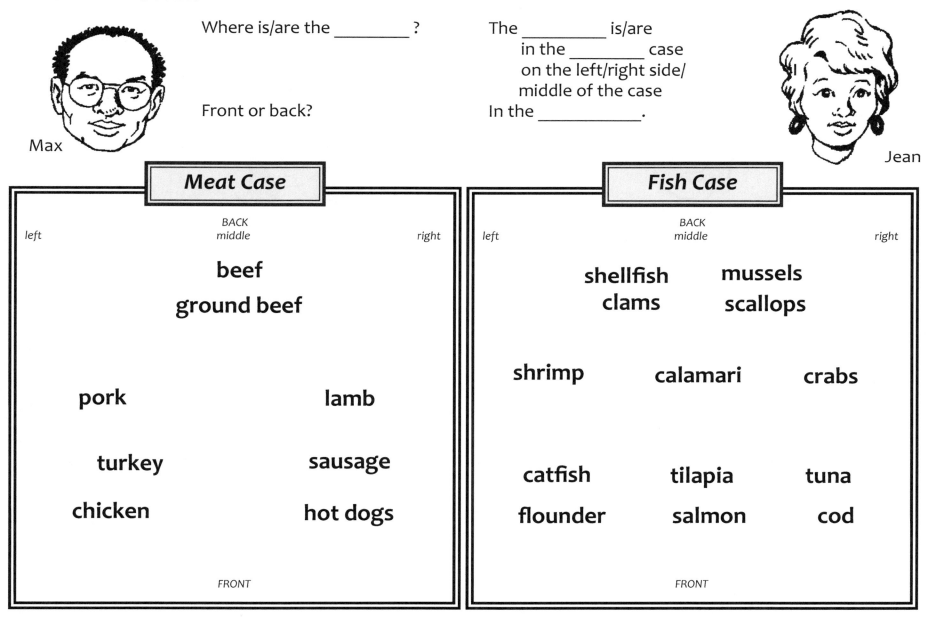

Max

Where is/are the _____ ?

Front or back?

The _____ is/are
in the _____ case
on the left/right side/
middle of the case
In the _____ .

Jean

Meat Case

left	BACK *middle*	*right*
	beef	
	ground beef	
pork		lamb
turkey		sausage
chicken		hot dogs
	FRONT	

Fish Case

left	BACK *middle*	*right*
shellfish	mussels	
clams	scallops	
shrimp	calamari	crabs
catfish	tilapia	tuna
flounder	salmon	cod
	FRONT	

LISTEN AND SAY

Jeff

Here's the seafood department.

I'm OK with seafood for tonight,

but how about meat for tomorrow?

How about salmon?

Sounds good.

Farm-raised is $8.99; wild-caught is $9.99.

And tomorrow we have meat, right?

I guess so, but I want thighs.

I know, but thighs taste better.

Jill

So, shall we get seafood or meat?

Right. So, what kind of fish?

OK with me.

Farm-raised or wild-caught?

I'm OK with farm-raised, but fresh, not frozen.

All right, but can we get chicken for a change?

Breast is better for you.

OK, OK. Then let's get a whole chicken.

TELL AND WRITE

What did they do?

went   seafood   _____

got   salmon   _____

what kind?   _____

did they get beef?   _____

did they get chicken?   _____

what kind?   _____

got   farm raised   _____

wanted   thighs   _____

got   whole chicken   _____

WRITE AND DO

Get a grocery store flyer and write down all the seafood and meat items.
Then write down the prices.

SEAFOOD	PRICE	MEAT	PRICE
_____	_____	_____	_____
_____	_____	_____	_____
_____	_____	_____	_____
_____	_____	_____	_____
_____	_____	_____	_____
_____	_____	_____	_____
_____	_____	_____	_____
_____	_____	_____	_____

LOOK AROUND AND DO IT

Go to seafood and/or meat department and make a map showing the items in the display.

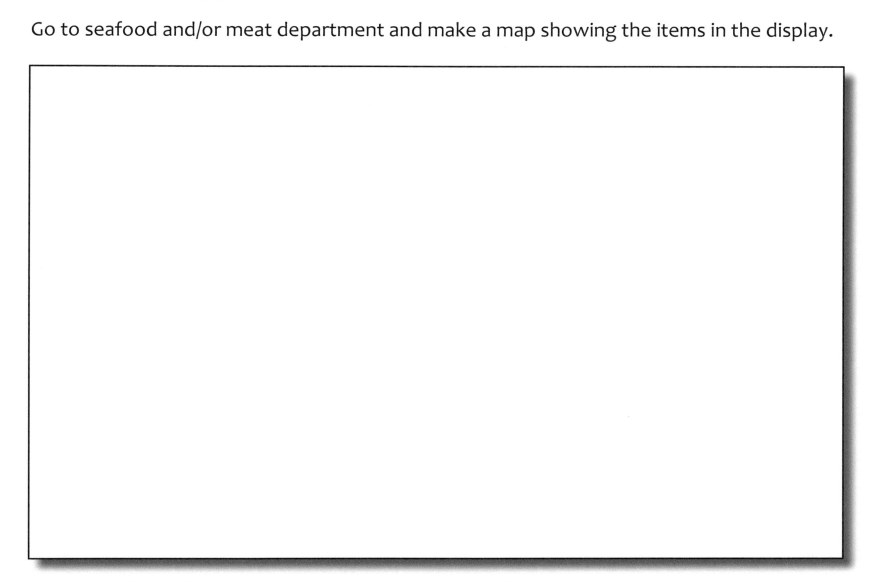

Note: It is advisable to explain to the department managers why you are doing this.

The Produce Department

VEGETABLES	
beets	carrots
lettuce	corn
spinach	potatoes
cabbage	tomatoes

FRUIT	
peaches	pears
oranges	grapes
grapefruit	melons
apples	bananas

READ

The produce department is very big.
There are many kinds of fruit and vegetables.
Many items are sold by the pound.

There are scales for weighing them.

There are also nuts and berries.
Strawberries and blueberries are very popular.
Blueberries are very nutritious.

The nuts are sold in bulk.
You get a scoop to take them
    out of a container
    and put them in a bag.
Then you put a label on the bag.

PLU #
1358

You may also find salad dressing and croutons here.

And don't forget the parsley and other herbs.

ANSWER

1. How big is the produce department? _____

2. What is in the produce department? _____

3. How are many items sold? _____

4. What are the scales for? _____

5. What berry is very nutritious? _____

6. How are the nuts sold? _____

7. How do you get the nuts? _____

8. What do you put on the bag? _____

9. What is parsley? _____

10. How many kinds of fruit are there? _____

LISTEN

Fern and Vern work in the produce department.
They have all kinds of produce.

I'm Fern. I manage the fruit section. We sell a lot of bananas and apples.
Some fruit is not so popular – for example, kiwis.

I'm Vern. I manage the vegetable section. We sell a lot of potatoes and tomatoes.
Some vegetables are not so popular – for example, kale.

Our co-worker Herb works with bulk items such as nuts.
He sells a lot of nuts, especially walnuts and almonds.
Dried apricots are also very popular. He sells a lot of them.

ANSWER

sells	fruit	vegetable	bananas
manages	popular	kale	
co-worker	bulk	almonds	
dried	nuts	section	

1. Fern _____ the _____ section.

2. _____ are in the fruit _____.

3. Apples are very _____.

4. Vern manages the _____ section.

5. Herb is their _____ .

6. Walnuts and _____ are _____.

7. _____ apricots are not fresh.

8. Herb sells _____ items.

9. Vern _____ a lot of tomatoes and potatoes, but not much _____.

ASK AND ANSWER

Lou

Where is/are the ___?   The ___ is/are

next to the ____
on the ____ side
in the middle
in back of/in front of ____

Fern

Produce Department

left

BACK
middle

right

cherries	potatoes	cabbage
grapes	onions	lettuce
pears	peppers	carrots
peaches	tomatoes	beets
apples		asparagus
bananas	oranges	corn
melons	grapefruit	spinach

FRONT

LISTEN AND SAY

Lou

Let's get the produce first.
We need potatoes.

Five pounds of potatoes?

Right. Where are they?

Ah, yes. How many?

It's over there, on the right side.

We don't need carrots.

Let's get one package.

Yes. Dried cranberries and walnuts.

OK. Now let's go to the dairy department.

Ruth

OK. I'll push the cart.

I think so. I can weigh them.
What about peppers?

Behind the tomatoes.

Just two, but we also need corn.

I'll get it and put it in the cart.
Carrots are there too.

What about lettuce?

Done. Anything else?

The dried fruit is over there. I'll get the walnuts.
Half a pound?

TELL AND WRITE

Who did what? Ruth or They?

got	produce	*Th* _____
pushed	cart	*R* _____
weighed	potatoes	*R* _____
got	corn	*R* _____
put	cart	*R* _____
didn't need	carrots	*Th* _____
got	one package	*Th* _____
got	walnuts	*R* _____

WRITE AND DO

Get a grocery store flyer and write down all the fruit and vegetable items and their prices. Then take turns asking and answering "How much is/are _____?"

FRUIT	PRICE (per pound, each)	VEGETABLES	PRICE (per pound, each)
_____	_____	_____	_____
_____	_____	_____	_____
_____	_____	_____	_____
_____	_____	_____	_____
_____	_____	_____	_____
_____	_____	_____	_____
_____	_____	_____	_____
_____	_____	_____	_____
_____	_____	_____	_____
_____	_____	_____	_____
_____	_____	_____	_____

LOOK AROUND AND DO IT

Go to a produce department and make a map showing the items in the display.

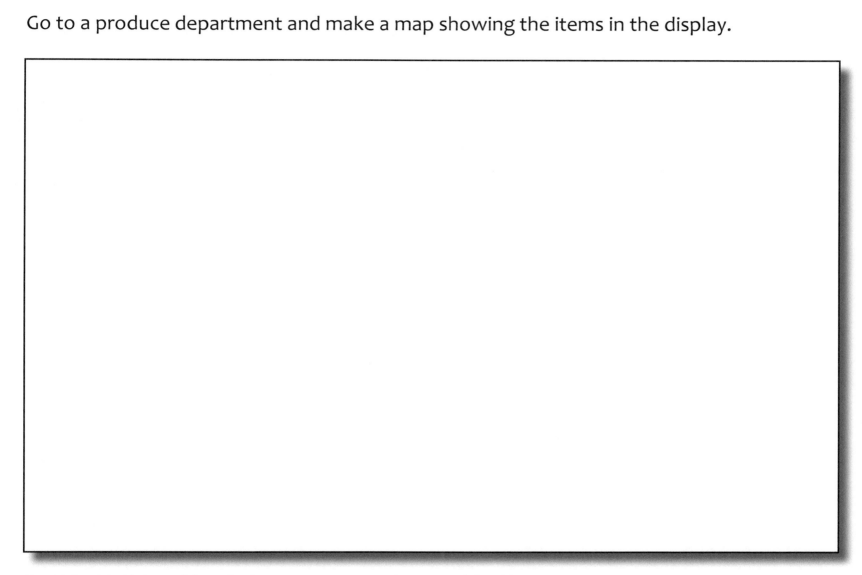

Note: It is advisable to explain to the department managers why you are doing this.

The Dairy and Frozen Food Departments

DAIRY & FROZEN FOOD

whole milk	2% milk	cream	half and half
gallon	half-gallon	quart	pint half pint
grated cheese	Swiss cheese	cheddar cheese	yogurt
sliced cheese	butter	margarine	ice cream

READ

The dairy department is on the left side of the store.
Dairy products are kept cool in refrigerated cases.
Most things are sold in packages. Milk is sold in cartons.

There are many kinds of cheese. Some cheese is sliced.
Some cheese is grated. Some is domestic and some is imported.

Ice cream is a dairy product, but it is sold in the frozen foods department.
The frozen foods department is next to the dairy department.

There are many kinds of ice cream. Popular kinds are vanilla, chocolate, and strawberry.

In the frozen foods cases there are many kinds of frozen foods.

Pizza is very popular. There are many kinds of frozen vegetables and fruit,
and there are many kinds of complete dinners.

ANSWER

1. Where is the dairy department? _____

2. How are dairy products sold? _____

3. How is milk sold? _____

4. Is Vermont cheddar cheese domestic or imported? _____

5. Is yoghurt a dairy product? _____

6. Is ice cream a dairy product? _____

7. Where do you find ice cream? _____

8. Where is the frozen food department? _____

9. What can you get in the frozen food department? _____

10. Is pizza a dairy product? _____

LISTEN

Beth

Hi. My name is Beth.

I work in the dairy department.

All the dairy products are kept cold.

You can get butter in the dairy department.

You can also get non-dairy spreads.

Margarine is a non-dairy spread.

We have many kinds of cheese.

My co-worker Bess works in the frozen food department.

All the products there are frozen.

Bess has many flavors of ice cream.

Vanilla is my favorite.

Some yogurt is also frozen.

Bess sells a lot of pizza.

In fact, all kinds of food can be frozen.

Bess

ANSWER

dairy   frozen   cheese
products   cold   kept
flavors   butter   ice cream
vanilla   yogurt   margarine

1. Yogurt is _____ in the dairy department.

2. _____ is a non-dairy product.

3. _____, _____, _____, and _____ are dairy products.

4. Ice cream needs to be _____ .

5. Beth works in the _____ department.

6. Dairy _____ need to be kept cold.

7. _____ and chocolate are _____ of ice cream.

8. Cheese needs to be kept _____ .

ASK AND ANSWER

Paul

Where is/are the _____?

Where in the _____?

The _____ is/are in the _____.

in the _____.

to the left/right of the _____.

on the _____ side.

Bess

Cooler

left	BACK middle	right
sliced cheese	**butter**	**milk**
		gallons
		half-gallons
packaged cheese	**non-dairy spreads**	**quarts**
		pints
		cream
cheddar cheese	**cottage cheese**	
		half & half

FRONT

Freezer

left	BACK middle	right	
	ICE CREAM		
gallons	**half-gallons**	**quarts**	**pints**
vanilla ice cream	**strawberry ice cream**	**chocolate ice cream**	
fruit	**frozen yogurt**	**dinners**	
vegetables		**pizza**	
	juice		

FRONT

LISTEN AND SAY

Mike

Vern

Mike	Vern
Here we are in the frozen foods aisle.	The only thing we need here is ice cream.
Strawberry this week?	Why not vanilla? We just had strawberry.
Oh, yeah. Would you like to have chocolate?	Sure. Half-gallon?
Are you sure that's enough?	It's enough. Let's go to dairy.
Next aisle. Have we got enough milk?	About a quart. We'll need milk. How about butter?
We've got enough. But we need sliced cheese.	Aha! There it is. Anything else?
Done. Let's go to the checkout.	

TELL AND WRITE

What did they do?

needed	ice cream	_____
just had	strawberry	_____
wanted	chocolate	_____
got	half-gallon	_____
were	sure	_____
got	milk	_____
needed	sliced cheese	_____
went	checkout	_____

WRITE AND DO

Write down your favorite dairy items and frozen food. # 1 is most favorite
Compare with a friend.

MY TOP TEN

Dairy	*Frozen Food*
1 _____	1 _____
2 _____	2 _____
3 _____	3 _____
4 _____	4 _____
5 _____	5 _____
6 _____	6 _____
7 _____	7 _____
8 _____	8 _____
9 _____	9 _____
10 _____	10 _____

LOOK AROUND AND DO IT

Go to the dairy department and make a map of the showcase showing these items: yogurt, cheese, butter and spreads, and milk.

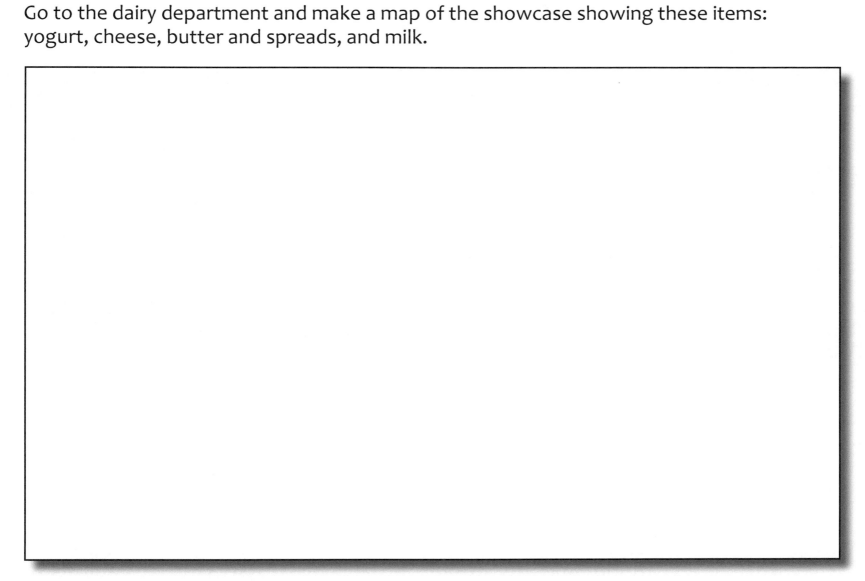

Note: It is advisable to explain to the department managers why you are doing this.

The Bakery and Deli

The Bakery and Deli

takeout	oven	display case	bread	pastry
domestic	sliced	filling	imported	pie
icing	turnover	cake	loaf	bagel
cookie	doughnut	roll	pasta	coleslaw

READ

Large supermarkets usually have a bakery and a deli. Although all baked goods and deli items are takeout, there may be a small place for eating the products in the store.

Large ovens in the bakery produce a variety of baked goods, and the wonderful smell of fresh-baked bread is in the air. The bakery can produce a wide variety of breads, such as wheat, rye, and bagels. For the customers with a sweet tooth, there are many kinds of baked goods: cakes, pies, cookies, and pastries. Some pastries have fruit fillings and some have colorful icing.

Bread is sold by the loaf, and items such as doughnuts and cookies are sold by the half-dozen or dozen. Bagels can also be sold as dozens.

The deli display cases have a very big selection of cheeses, both domestic and imported. Cheeses from France and Italy are very popular. The deli also has many kinds of special meat in large loaves. The cheese and meat are sold sliced and by the pound.

ANSWER

1. Where are the large ovens? _____

2. What does the bakery produce? _____

3. How is bread sold? _____

4. How are cookies sold? _____

5. What are pastries? _____

6. What is sold by the pound? _____

7. What is sold sliced? _____

LISTEN

Hi again. It's me, Chuck. I want to tell you about our bakery and our delicatessen. We call it the "deli."

Howie manages the deli. He has a wonderful variety of meats, cheeses, and salads.

The display cases are full of delicious cheeses from around the world. Our most popular imported cheeses are from France. The meats are displayed as large round packages, like loaves. You can have Howie cut off slices from the loaves. If you like salami, our house brand is really nice. We have fresh pasta salads, and our coleslaw is very popular.

Howie   Jane

Jane is our head baker. Her ovens are always busy producing many kinds of breads and rolls. And I think our pastries are as good as any in town. You should try our turnovers. My favorite has strawberry filling. Jane's bagels are very popular with our customers. We sell a lot.

ANSWER

baked   manages   imported   meats

slices   baker   brand

turnover   loaves   cases

1. Howie _____ the deli.

2. The display _____ are full of cheeses and _____.

3. French cheese is _____.

4. The meat is sold as _____.

5. Chuck thinks the house _____ salami is really nice.

6. The head _____ is Jane.

7. _____ bread smells great.

8. The meats are packaged as _____, like bread.

9. A _____ is a kind of pastry.

ASK AND ANSWER

Put these cheese, bakery, and meat items in the right place, and then ask and answer.

rye bread	Swiss	chocolate cake	roquefort
oatmeal cookies	salami	strawberry turnovers	honey ham
apple pie	onion bagels	cheddar	baloney

Meat Case	Cheese Case	Bakery

Hugh

Excuse me, where can I find _____ ?

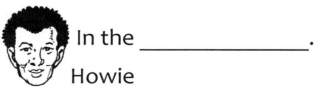

Howie

In the _____ .

LISTEN AND SAY

Howie

Hugh

Hey, Hugh, can I help you?

I need to make some sandwiches for a picnic. So I guess I'll go with sliced ham and cheese.

Good choice. How much ham?

A pound should do it.

Swiss cheese goes well with ham.

Sounds good.

Thick sliced or thin?

Thin, please.

Like this?

Perfect.

And I recommend Jane's rye bread.

TELL AND WRITE

What did they say?

Howie: help _____

Hugh: needed _____

Howie: asked how much _____

Hugh: should _____

Howie: goes well _____

Howie: asked _____

Hugh: said _____

Howie: recommended _____

WRITE AND DO

Describe the steps for making a ham and Swiss sandwich and a peanut butter and jelly sandwich. Then make a sandwich.

HAM AND SWISS

1 get _____

2 put _____

3 put _____

PEANUT BUTTER AND JELLY

1 get _____

2 spread _____

3 spread _____

4 put _____

LOOK AROUND AND DO IT

Go to a deli and make a list of at least ten meats and cheeses.

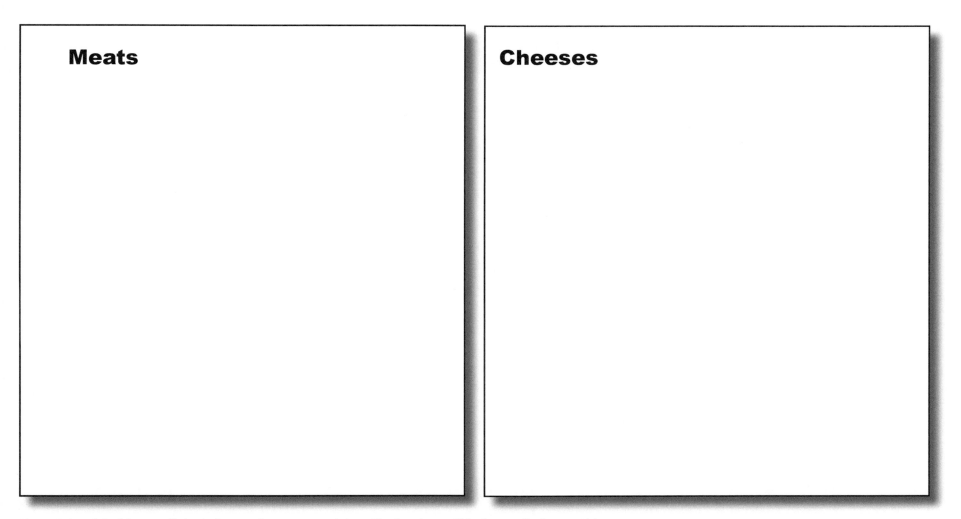

Meats	**Cheeses**

Note: *It is advisable to tell the helpers what you are doing. Maybe they will help you find everything.*

The Convenience Store

CONVENIENCE STORE

neighborhood	newspaper	soft drinks	beer	convenient
gas station	candy	deli	snacks	bags of ice
sandwiches	soup	campfire wood	coffee	road maps
restroom	milk	lottery tickets	newspaper	

READ

A convenience store is a small neighborhood store.

It is usually also a gas station. It may have a small deli inside.

The deli may sell sandwiches, soup, and salads.

There may not be a place to sit and eat. The food is for takeout.

People often stop for a newspaper or a road map or a lottery ticket.

They also buy a lot of milk, soft drinks, beer, and coffee.

The store also sells snacks and candy.

The prices in a convenience store are higher than at a supermarket.

There may be restrooms for customers.

A similar place is a rest area on a main highway. Large rest areas have different kinds
of fast food, places to sit and eat, and restrooms. Small rest areas have only restrooms
and vending machines.

ANSWER

1. How big is a convenience store? _____

2. What does the store usually sell outside the store? _____

3. Who can use the restrooms? _____

4. What kinds of drinks can you buy? _____

6. What can you get at the deli? _____

7. What non-food items can you find at the store? _____

8. How are the prices at a convenience store? _____

9. Where do you find rest areas? _____

10. How is a large rest area different from a convenience store? _____

LISTEN

Hi. My name is Joe.

I work in a convenience store.

I am the cashier.

I have a key to the restrooms.

My friend Martha has a small deli. She makes

sandwiches, soups, and other takeout food.

Sometimes people come in for just one thing –

a newspaper, a coffee, a quart of milk, or a

six-pack of beer.

They also buy lottery tickets.

I live near the store. It is the only store

in my neighborhood.

So, it's very convenient.

ANSWER

restrooms   non-food   rest areas
price   takeout   neighborhood
cigarettes   soft drinks   six-pack

1. People often buy a _____ of beer.

2. You cannot eat our food here; it is _____ only.

3. The _____ of milk is higher here.

4. Some people stop to get a pack of _____ .

5. A lottery ticket is a _____ item.

6. The store sells a lot of _____ like cola.

7. On a main highway you will find _____ .

   There are _____ there.

9. The store is in Joe's _____ .

ASK AND ANSWER

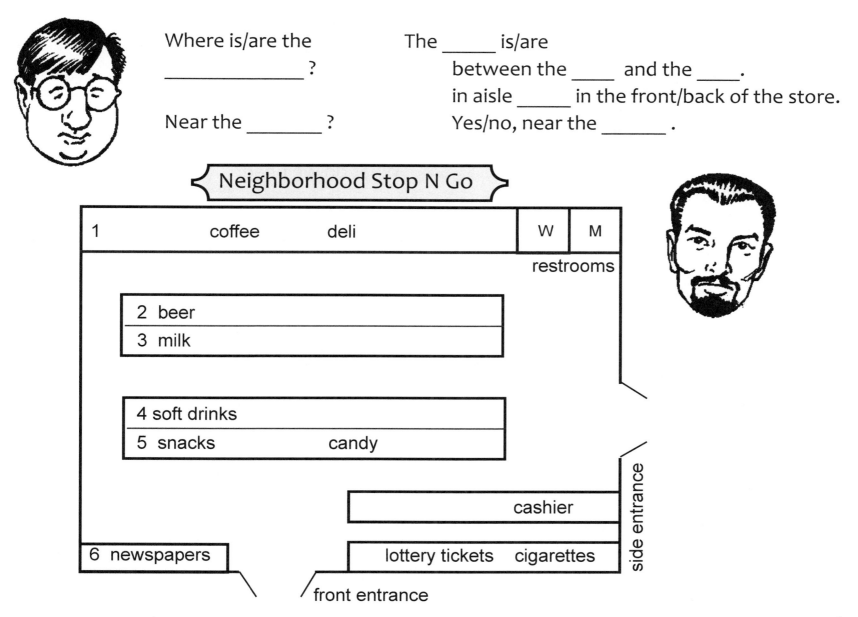

Where is/are the

_____ ?

Near the _____ ?

The _____ is/are

between the _____ and the _____.

in aisle _____ in the front/back of the store.

Yes/no, near the _____ .

Neighborhood Stop N Go

1	coffee	deli

W | M

restrooms

2 beer

3 milk

4 soft drinks

5 snacks   candy

cashier

6 newspapers

lottery tickets   cigarettes

side entrance

front entrance

LISTEN AND SAY

Jane  Howie

Jane	Howie
Before we go home, let's stop at the Neighborhood Stop N Go.	What do we need?
We're almost out of milk.	Oh, yeah. And I should get some beer.
Look! Gas is cheaper here than at FastStop.	You're right. That is a good price. But we don't need gas.
OK. So here we are! Shall I wait in the car?	OK, but give me some money.
How come? Don't you have your STOP N GO card?	I want to pay with cash.
How much?	A twenty should do it.
Here. I guess I'll use the restroom, after all.	I think I'll get some snacks, and a BINGO ticket.
Just one!	Of course!

TELL AND WRITE

What did they do?

stopped	Stop N Go	_____
needed	milk	_____
got	beer	_____
didn't need	gas	_____
didn't wait	car	_____
asked for	money	_____
wanted	to pay	_____
how much	want	_____
used	restroom	_____
got	snacks, ticket	_____

WRITE AND DO

Make a list of your favorite drinks and snacks and compare with your classmates.
Then write about each person's favorites.

MY FAVORITES   _____'S FAVORITES

Drinks   ### Drinks

1 _____   1 _____

2 _____   2 _____

3 _____   3 _____

4 _____   4 _____

Snacks   ### Snacks

1 _____   1 _____

2 _____   2 _____

3 _____   3 _____

4 _____   4 _____

LOOK AROUND AND DO IT

Stop at a convenience store and compare its plan with the plan on page 57.
Then make a map of the convenience store. If the cashier isn't busy, ask them what they sell.
Ask about customers' favorites.

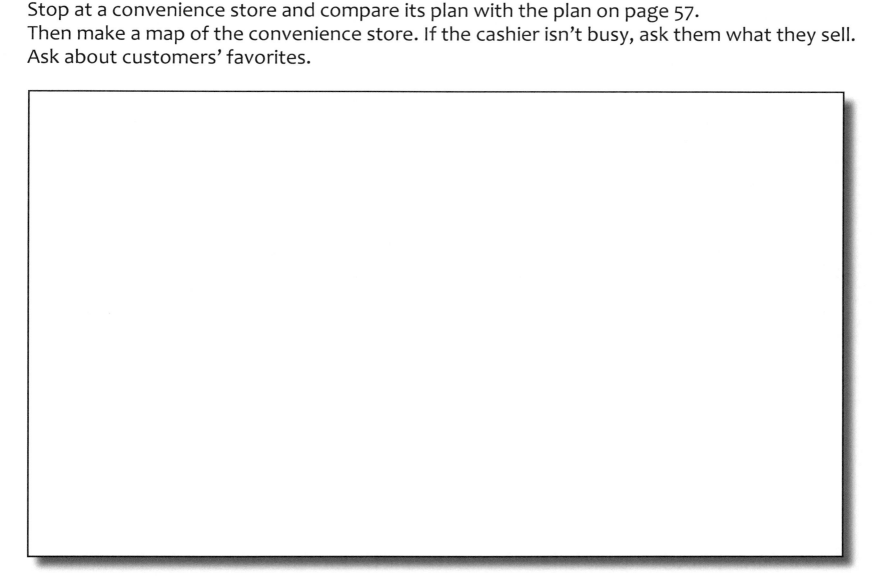

Note: It is advisable to explain to the department managers why you are doing this.

The Drug Store/Pharmacy

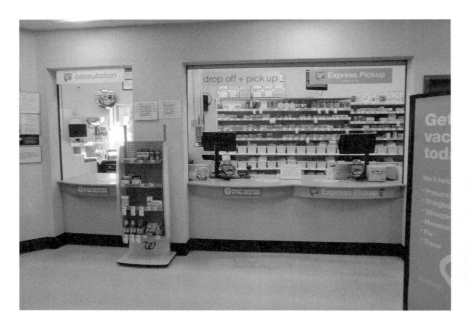

THE DRUG STORE

chain	over-the-counter (OTC)	antacids	eye care
pharmacy	prescription	laxatives	foot care
pharmacist	refill	dietary supplements	hair care
magazines	pills	vitamins	conditioner
one-hour photo	pain killer	beauty products	shampoo

READ

The drugstore sells many things.

One part of the store is the pharmacy. A pharmacist works in the pharmacy.

Pharmacists prepare prescription drugs. A doctor writes a prescription.

Some prescription drugs can be refilled when you need more. Some cannot.

Many drugs are sold without a prescription.

These drugs are called OTC or over-the-counter drugs.

There are many types of these non-prescription drugs. Some pain killers are OTC drugs.

And we carry vitamins and other dietary supplements.

Most drug stores sell many other products. Some are for eye care, foot care, skin care, and hair care (shampoo and conditioner). They also sell a little of everything, including magazines and greeting cards. Some may do photo processing.

Many drug stores are part of national chains such as Walgreens, Rite-Aid, and CVS.

ANSWER

1. What does a drug store sell?

2. Who works in a pharmacy?

3. What does the pharmacy sell?

4. Who writes a prescription and who prepares the prescription drugs?

5. Can you refill a prescription?

6. Are some drugs sold without a prescription?

   What do we call these drugs?

7. What kind of non-prescription drug is aspirin?

8. What kind of drug is a vitamin pill?

9. What is one example of a chain drug store?

10. What other non-food items can you find at the drug store?

11. Do drug stores do photo processing?

LISTEN

Hello. My name is Lou.
I manage the Rex-Aid Drug Store.
We sell many things, including prescription drugs.

My name is Ruth. I am a pharmacist. I also work in the Rex-Aid Drug Store. I fill prescriptions, and I also do refills. A doctor writes the prescription and sends it to me. Sometimes a person brings the prescription to the pharmacy.

I'm Brooke. I am an employee. We sell many different kinds of medicine. We sell a lot of OTC medicine. I also do photo processing, and I can take your passport photo.

ANSWER

chain	pharmacist	pharmacy
over the counter	pain killer	fills
antacid	foot	eye
hair	vitamin	

1. I have a problem with my foot. Go to the _____ care section.

2. I have a problem with my eyes. Go to the _____ care section.

3. I need to shampoo my hair. Go to the _____ care section.

4. I have a pain. Get a _____ .

5. I have a prescription. Go to the _____ .

6. There are many stores in the Rex-Aid _____ .

7. Aspirin is an _____ medicine.

8. For acid stomach take an _____ .

9. A _____ _____ prescriptions.

10. I take a multi-_____ pill every day.

ASK AND ANSWER

Use the map of a drug store below and place several items on it. Then ask and answer with a partner.

Where is/are the
_____ ?

Did you say _____?

The _____ is/are
in the middle of aisle _____ .
at the end of aisle _____ .
in the front/back of the store.
on the left/right side of aisle _____ .

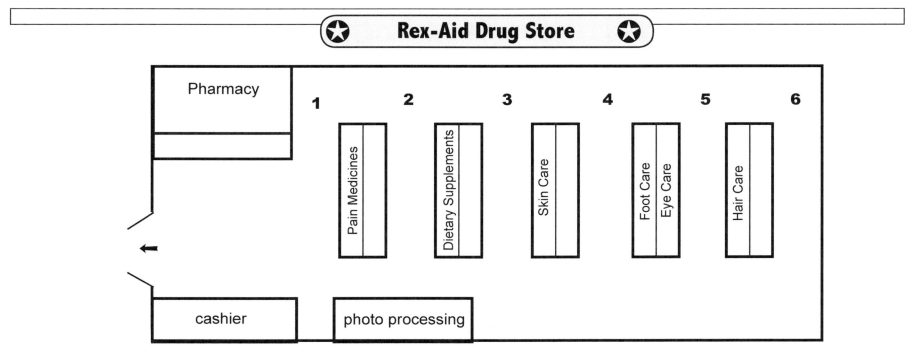

LISTEN AND SAY THIS PHONE CONVERSATION

Rrrrrrrrrrrring

Hi Fern, it's me. I'll be home a little late today.

Well, I have to stop at Rex-Aid.
I saw Doctor Aslan for my RLS problem.

She gave me a prescription.

I don't know. She called it in,
but I forgot the name.

All right. Anything else?

Yeah, we do.

Good idea.

OK. Let's see: prescription, vitamin D,
shampoo, photos and …… uhmmmm

Hello?

How come?

What for?
So, what did she say?

What is it?

OK, but since you're going
there, could you get something
for me? I'm out of vitamin B-12.

Umm, yes, I think we need shampoo.

They have frozen foods there. Why
don't you pick up a pizza?
One more thing. Would you pick up
some photos for me?

PIZZA!

Beth

Fern

TELL AND WRITE

What did they do?

said   home late   _____

had to stop   at Rex-Aid   _____

saw   Dr. Aslan   _____

gave   prescription   _____

called   it   _____

forgot   name   _____

thought   needed   _____

picked up   photos   _____

WRITE AND DO

Find a drug store flyer and write down 10 items you need and their prices

Shopping List

NEED	PRICE
_____	_____
_____	_____
_____	_____
_____	_____
_____	_____
_____	_____
_____	_____
_____	_____
_____	_____

LOOK AROUND AND DO IT

Go to a drug store and compare its plan with the plan on page 67.
Then make a map of the drug store. If the cashier isn't busy, ask her what
she sells a lot of. Ask about customers' favorites.

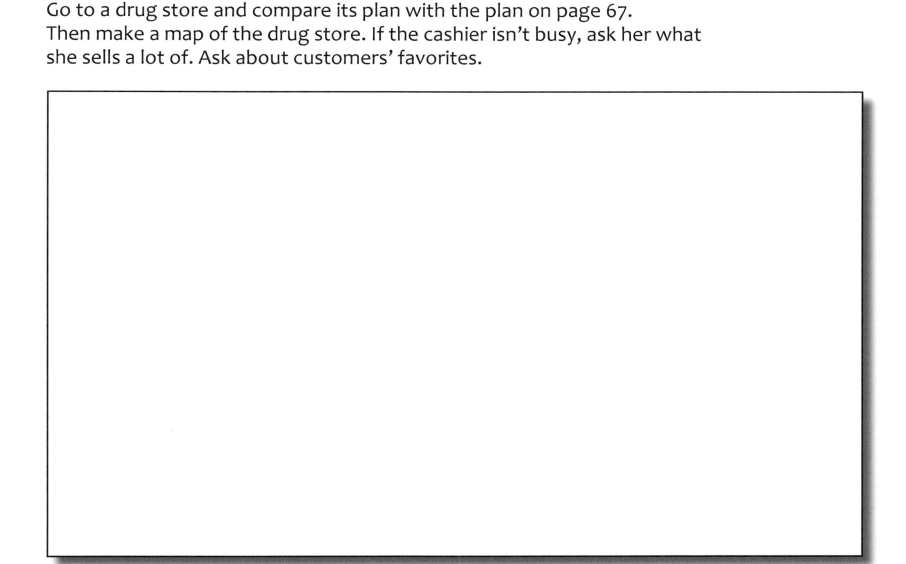

Note: It is advisable to explain to the store manager why you are doing this.

THE GAS STATION

The Gas Station

gas tank	credit	to pump	empty	debit	to replace
full serve	to choose	receipt	self-serve	cheapest	car wash
attendant	grade	pump	per gallon	cash	gas cap
		charge	nozzle		

READ

Jill and Jeff need to get gas for their car.

The gas tank is almost empty. They will drive to a gas station.

At the station a sign says SELF SERVE. They need to put the gas in the tank.

No one will help.

Some stations offer full service. An attendant will put in the gas.

Which side is the gas cap on? Left or right? It's on the left.

They will drive to the right of the pump.

They will need to choose cash or charge. The card can be for credit or debit.

Debit means the money is automatically charged to their account.

They will choose cash. Jeff goes into the station. He gives $15.00 to the cashier.

Jill chooses regular gas, the cheapest grade. The cost is shown as per gallon.

She removes the gas cap. She removes the nozzle. She pumps the gas until it stops at $15.00.

She replaces the nozzle and the gas cap.

She gets a receipt at the pump. They decide to drive through the car wash.

Then they go home.

ANSWER

1. What do Jill and Jeff need?

2. Where do they need to go ?

3. What does the sign say?

4. Which side is the cap on?

5. Which do they choose, cash or credit?

6. How much gas does Jeff pay for?

7. Who pumps the gas?

8. How much does she pump?

9. Who gets the receipt?

10. Then what do they do?

LISTEN

Hello. My name is Max.
I own TopGas. It is a gas station.
It is a franchise. I own the store, but
it is part of a chain. I pay part of my sales
to the chain. I can use the chain's name.

This place is also a convenience store. We sell a lot of gas, but we make a lot of sales inside the store. A lot of our sales are in the morning and late afternoon.

People rush in for coffee in the morning. Sometimes they pick up a breakfast snack or a sandwich for lunch at our deli. In the evening, they rush in to get milk or beer to take home.

I sell a lot of things, but none of my sales are very big.

ANSWER

chain	owner	pick up	makes
rush in	franchise	inside	snacks

1. In the morning we sell sandwiches and _____ .

2. TopGas is a _____, part of a _____.

3. The _____ is Max.

4. In the evening people _____ for milk or beer.

5. Some people _____ a sandwich for lunch.

6. His store _____ a lot of small sales.

7. There is a deli _____ the store.

ASK AND ANSWER

This is a typical gas pump. You push a button to choose regular gas (87 octane – $2.37 per gallon), mid-grade (89 octane – $3.69), or premium (91 octane – %$3.07). The prices go up and down. All the gas is unleaded. In most states you can pump your own gas. You can pay cash inside the station for the amount of gas you want or use a credit or debit card at the pump and get a receipt. The nozzle is on the right.

 Jeff

 Jill

How much is the ____ grade?	It's _____ per gallon
Which grade shall we get?	Let's get _____ .
How many gallons?	Let's _____ .
Cash or charge?	Let's _____ .
Will you pump or pay?	I'll _____ .

LISTEN AND SAY

Max

Hi, Howie, I guess you're here for
   your usual coffee.

Any gas today?

Cash or charge?

OK. Insert the card.

Debit or credit?

OK, put in your PIN.

How about lunch?

Howie

Hey, Max. Gotta have that caffeine.

Yeah, I'll need twenty dollars.

Charge today.

Done.

Debit.

Done.

You bet. I want Martha's Italian sub
   and a cup of minestrone soup.

Joy

Hi, Howie. What's up?

You want to pick up the usual tuna and tomato?

Good choice. Give me a minute.

Howie, your order is ready.

Five-fifty plus tax.

Hi, Joy.

No, today I'll go Italian sub and
   minestrone.

Great. How much?

TELL AND WRITE

What did Howie do?

had to have	caffeine	_____
needed	gas	_____
charged	with debit	_____
inserted	card	_____
put in	PIN	_____
wanted	Italian	_____
picked up	cup	_____
paid	plus	_____

WRITE AND DO

Look at the gas stations on the map below and write their locations.

North

```
                                           High Street
   West                                                                          East
          3                    4
          8                    5              7
                    Hill Street    River Street
                    Main Street
          2                    6   Cross Street   1
```

South

1 Sunoco   *Sunoco is on the southeast corner of Main and Cross Streets.*

2 Gulf   _____

3 Getty   _____

4 BP   _____

5 Mobil   _____

6 CITGO   _____

7 Shell   _____

8 TopGas   _____

LOOK AROUND AND DO IT

Go around town to compare gas prices at several gas stations. Write them below:

Station	Regular	Mid	Premium
_____	_____	_____	_____
_____	_____	_____	_____
_____	_____	_____	_____
_____	_____	_____	_____
_____	_____	_____	_____
_____	_____	_____	_____
_____	_____	_____	_____
_____	_____	_____	_____
_____	_____	_____	_____

Then compare prices with some other part of the country. For example, go to the internet and Google <gas prices Dallas, Texas>

THE THRIFT SHOP

The Thrift Shop

jacket	coat	gloves	to try on	T-shirts
housewares	affordable	inexpensive	sandals	condition
sweater	furniture	to fit	shorts	boots

READ

Jean and her two children need some clothes. It is summer and the children have summer clothes. They have shorts and T-shirts.

Soon it will be fall. They will need warmer clothes. They will go to school. They need jackets, shirts, and pants and sweaters. By November they will need winter clothes: hats, coats, and gloves.

They go to Downtown Thrift. It sells affordable clothes, housewares, furniture, and other things. These things are all used but most of the items are in good condition. And they are inexpensive.

Jean would like to have a new dress. She sees a very pretty green and red dress. She would like to try it on. She goes to the fitting room and puts it on. It is too large; she needs a smaller one. She sees a nice skirt for her daughter.

She looks at some shoes. Her sandals will not be warm enough for the fall weather. She tries on a pair of walking shoes. They fit her very well, and they are not worn. They look new. And only $7.50. Then she looks for boots for the children. There are not many boots. Maybe there will be more next month.

ANSWER

1. What do Jean and her children need?

2. Why do they need it?

3. What kind of clothes do they need?

4. Where do they go?

5. What does this place sell?

6. Are the items new or used?

7. What would Jean like to have?

8. What does she try on? Does it fit?

9. How do the walking shoes fit?

10. Does she buy boots for the children?

LISTEN

Hi, My name is Jill.

I am the general manager of Downtown Thrift. I have several helpers. Some are part-time. They work only a few hours each week.

We sell lots of things. People give us things they do not need or want. Most things are used. Some are new. Because they are used, or second-hand, we sell them at affordable prices.

We are a non-profit store. We give our "profit" to charities. For example, we give money to children's clubs. We give money to homeless shelters and other organizations that help the poor and elderly.

We sell many different things, but clothing is our biggest seller. Many college students buy their clothes here. Many shoppers are mothers with children. Growing children need a lot of clothes as they grow bigger. We have lots and lots of very inexpensive toys and games.

JJ is my assistant. She is in charge of the housewares and furniture sections. When people move away, we get lots of donations, such as pots and pans and chairs. When new people come to town, they often get many of these inexpensive things for their homes.

ANSWER

used	try on	fitting	part-time
condition	housewares	affordable	donations
inexpensive	non-profit	charity	furniture

1. The jacket was in good _____. There was nothing wrong with it.

2. You _____ clothes in a _____ room.

3. _____ means it does not cost a lot. In other words it is _____.

4. A thrift shop sells mostly _____ clothes.

5. _____ are things like dishes, pots, and pans.

6. This thrift shop is _____. It gives its "profit" to a _____.

7. The shop gets its goods from _____.

8. A chair is a piece of _____.

9. She works _____, only 10 hours per week.

ASK AND ANSWER

Use: I ... me... my... you... your... she ... her ... we....them

 Jean

 Jill

Excuse _____, are _____ the manager?

Yes, _____ am. How can _____ help _____?

Do _____ take donations?

Yes, _____ do.

Good! Where do _____ leave _____?

At the side door, over there to _____ left.

_____, see. When can _____ bring _____?

Wednesdays and Thursdays.

By the way, does JJ work here?

Yes, _____ does, but _____ isn't here today.
Do _____ know _____?

Yes, _____'s my student. How's _____ doing?

_____'s a very good worker.

That's good to hear. Tell _____, Mrs. Miller said hello.

_____'ll do that.

Thank _____, and thanks for _____ time.

No problem.

LISTEN AND SAY

Jean

Jon, let's not go to the mall.
Well, we can save money
by going to a thrift shop.

Downtown Thrift.
No, it's on South Main.

And it's non-profit. They give some of
their sales money to charities.
Neighborhood Kid's Playce.

You can find some really nice
things there – even used furniture.

They have lots and lots of
books, toys, and games.

Jon

Why not?

Which one?

The one on Flat Street?
Oh, yeah. I've seen their sign.

Such as?
That's good, but are the clothes OK?

And I need a small table for my office.
Do they have stuff for the kids?

TELL AND WRITE

What do you think they did at the thrift shop?

went	thrift shop	_____
saved	money	_____
looked at	?	_____
picked up	?	_____
found	?	_____
bought	?	_____
spent	?	_____

WRITE AND DO

What is the name of your nearest thrift shop?

_____

Where is it?

_____

What do they sell?

_____

How many people work there?

_____

Are they volunteers?

_____

What charities does it support?

_____

LOOK AROUND AND DO IT

Go to a thrift shop. Look at several things and write their names and prices below.

Item	Price	Item	Price
_____	_____	_____	_____
_____	_____	_____	_____
_____	_____	_____	_____
_____	_____	_____	_____
_____	_____	_____	_____
_____	_____	_____	_____
_____	_____	_____	_____
_____	_____	_____	_____
_____	_____	_____	_____
_____	_____	_____	_____

Note: It is advisable to explain to the store manager why you are doing this.

The Hardware Store

The Hardware Store

tools	paint	hammer	paint brush	nail	flashlight	screwdriver
battery	screw	tape	nut and bolt	glue	wrench	broom
saw	brush	drill	sandpaper	dustpan		

READ

There are many things
in a hardware store.
There are many kinds of paint.
There are many colors of paint.

There are many kinds of tools.
There are hammers and screwdrivers.
Nails, screws, nuts, and bolts
connect things.

Hammers pound nails into wood.
Screwdrivers drive screws into wood.
Nuts and bolts connect wood or metal.
A wrench tightens nuts.
A saw cuts things.

A flashlight is used to give light.
A flashlight needs batteries.
Tape and glue are used to fix things.
Brooms, brushes, and dustpans are used to clean the floor.

ANSWER

1. What's in a hardware store?

2. What does a hammer do?

3. What do screwdrivers do?

4. What does a wrench do?

5. What does a saw do?

6. What do tape and glue do?

7. What is a broom used for?

8. What is a flashlight used for?

9. What does a flashlight need?

LISTEN

Hi there!

My name is Jeff.
I work at Main Street Hardware.
There are many things in the store.
I know where everything is.
I like to help customers.
I can help you find things.
I like to say,
"If we don't have it,
you don't need it."

Of course, I will order it for you.

Take a cart or a basket
and tell me what you need.

We have four aisles.
Tools are in aisle 1, right side.
Nails, screws, nuts, and bolts
are also in aisle 1, left side.

Cleaning supplies are in aisle 2.
Other stuff is in aisle 2, right side.

Electrical and plumbing supplies
are in aisles 3 and 4,
and paint is in the back of the store.

ANSWER

tell	bolts	order
help	paint	electrical
supplies	find	take

1. _____ a basket and ask Jeff.

2. Jeff likes to _____ customers.

3. He can _____ everything.

4. Cleaning _____ are not in aisle 1.

5. _____ Jeff what you need.

6. If he doesn't have it, he will _____ it.

7. _____ and plumbing things are in aisles 3 and 4.

8. Nuts and _____ are in aisle 1.

9. _____ is in the back of the store.

ASK AND ANSWER

Brooke

Excuse me, where
can I find _____ ?

Thanks.

You'll find it/them
    in aisle _____.
    at the back _____.

Don't mention it.

Jeff

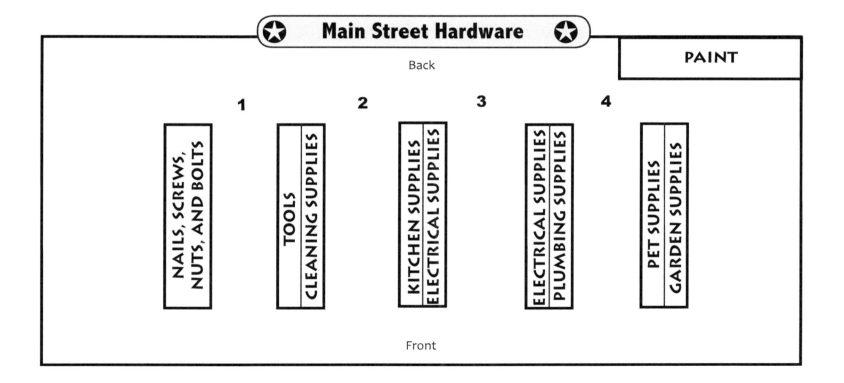

LISTEN AND SAY

Good afternoon.
How can I help you?
I can help.

Sure thing! Right down
aisle one. Follow me.

They're in aisle 3. Right side.

Cleaning supplies.

Aisle 2, left side.

Yes, halfway down the
aisle. We have all kinds.

My pleasure.
All kinds.

Good afternoon.
I need to get a few things.
Good. Can you tell me
where I can get a Phillips
screwdriver, and screws?

Thanks. . . .
Now where are the flashlights?

And a broom?

Where's that?

Can I find dish detergent there?

You've been very helpful. Thanks.

Oh, do you take credit cards?

TELL AND WRITE

What did Brooke and Jeff do?

needed   a few things   _____

told   where to get   screwdriver _____

followed   down aisle 1   _____

asked   flashlights   _____

told   aisle 2   _____

told   dish detergent _____

said   very helpful   _____

WRITE AND DO

Find out what all these things are and then write in the second and third columns what you have and do not have in your home.

	Have	Do not have
flashlight	_____	_____
batteries	_____	_____
screwdriver	_____	_____
hammer	_____	_____
wrench	_____	_____
saw	_____	_____
glue	_____	_____
smoke alarm	_____	_____
fire extinguisher	_____	_____
first aid kit	_____	_____
candles	_____	_____

LOOK AROUND AND DO IT

Go to a hardware store and make a map of where everything on page 92 is. Or tell what aisle these things are in.

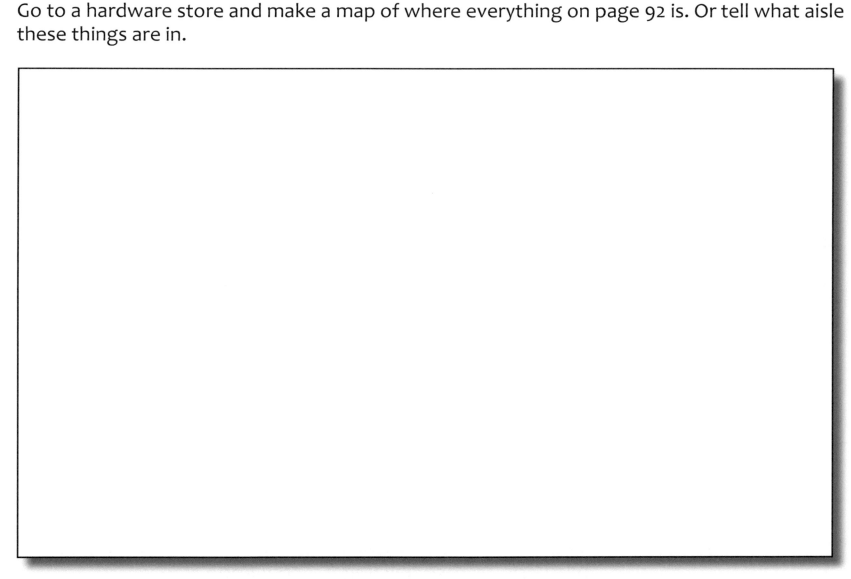

Note: It is advisable to tell the helpers what you are doing. Maybe they will help you find everything.

THE MALL

The Mall				
big box store	shops	to rest	vendors	hallway
electronics	kiosk	to watch	parking lot	comfort
clothing	bench	food court	safe	strollers
	bargains	socializing	challenge	

READ

There are many shops in a mall.

Many malls have a "big box" store at each end of the mall. At one end, the big store may sell electronics: for example, computers, cameras, phones, video games.

At the other end, there maybe a large clothing store.
It sells men's suits, jackets, pants, sweaters, and underwear. It also sells women's clothes: for example, dresses, skirts, as well as suits, jackets, pants, and sweaters.

Some large malls have several big box stores. Between these, there are large hallways that go down the middle of the building to each big box store. These hallways are also called malls. In the middle of these malls there may be kiosks that sell things such as cell phones. There may also be benches where people can sit and rest their feet or just watch the shoppers and do some socializing.

On each side of these malls there are many shops and usually a food court with many vendors. You can find all kinds of fast food there.

The mall has a large parking lot. It is free, and many people like this free and easy way to park and look for bargains. Older people like the mall because they feel it is a safe place. They can sit, watch, and walk in comfort.

ANSWER

1. Where do you find a "big box" store?

2. What do you find in an electronics store?

3. What do clothing stores sell?

4. What is on each side of the large hallway?

5. What is the large hallway called?

6. Where do you find a kiosk?

7. What might be sold in a kiosk?

8. What do you find in a food court?

9. Why do people like the parking lot?

10. Why do older people like to go to the mall?

LISTEN

Hello, I am Bert. I am 75 years old. I come here to the mall from time to time. Sometimes I meet some old friends here. We like to sit and talk and watch the shoppers.

There are many kinds of shoppers. There are women with children. Some of them are pushing their babies in strollers. Some people come with their friends or neighbors looking for good bargains and a chance to talk.

There are older couples. They may do some shopping and then go to the food court. And there are teenagers. Often there are several of them together in a group.

Socializing is a very important reason for coming to the mall. Old or young, it's a popular place. But online shopping is now a big challenge for malls.

ANSWER

kiosks	old	online
shops	safe	watch
strollers	kinds	court

1. Bert is 75 years _____.

2. He comes to the mall to _____ the shoppers.

3. There are many kinds of _____.

4. Mothers may be pushing their babies in _____.

5. There may be _____ in the aisle.

6. There are many _____ of food in the food _____ .

7. Older people think the mall is _____.

8. But _____ shopping is now a big challenge for malls.

ASK AND ANSWER

Look at the plan of the mall. Then practice asking and answering with a friend.

Fashion Fair	Luggage	Cell Phones	Children's Clothes	Eyewear	Music	Toys	Food Court	BIG ELECTRONICS
	Books	Jewelry	Kitchen	Entrance	Video Games	Shoes	Sports Clothes	Restaurant	

Bev

Excuse me, can you tell me where _____ is?

Is it on the left or right side?

Thank you.

I think it's between _____ and _____.

I'm pretty sure it's _____ .

Bert

LISTEN AND SAY

Bert

Hello, Mike. It's good to see _____.

How have _____ been?

Oh, _____ pretty good.

_____ fine. She didn't want to come today. Too many other things to do.

Sure does. I can't keep up with _____.

Will do. How's _____ son?

Again? _____ thought he was happy at SuperMart.

So are _____ and _____ wife moving there?

Mike

Bert! Same to you, _____ friend.

Not bad. What about _____?

How's _____ wife?

She keeps busy, doesn't _____?

Tell _____ I said hello.

Oh, _____ got a new job.

Well, _____ didn't pay very well. So _____ left. _____ new job is in Springfield.

_____ think so.

TELL AND WRITE

What did Bert and Mike do?

Bert

said	good
asked	how
wife	didn't want
asked	son
thought	happy
asked	move

_____

_____

_____

_____

_____

_____

Mike

said	same
asked	how
asked	wife
told	said
son	new job
said	in Springfield

_____

_____

_____

_____

_____

_____

WRITE AND DO

Go to the internet and look for your nearest mall.
Write the names of all the shops in the mall and write what they sell.

SHOP	SELLS
_____	_____
_____	_____
_____	_____
_____	_____
_____	_____
_____	_____
_____	_____
_____	_____
_____	_____

LOOK AROUND AND DO IT

Go to your nearest mall. Look at the mall plan at the entrance. Write down at least six places you want to visit. Then go there, look around, and ask, "What is your hottest item?"

1.

2.

3.

4.

5.

6.

7.

8.

Introduction for the Teacher

This book is a vocabulary development book for English language learners who are high-beginner to low-intermediate fluency with a vocabulary of at least 300 words. Although it may be used occasionally as a photocopyable text, it may not be copied in its entirety as a book. It is recommended that each student have a copy of the book to use as a workbook and that you proceed through the text from Unit One to Unit Eleven. An audio CD is available to add a more effective listening component to the use of the text.

Each unit has ten activities. Fifteen to twenty key words are featured in each unit, resulting in a total of 213 words that are indexed on page 115. The key words are also listed in the table of contents pages, which can serve as a checklist as the students proceed through the text and demonstrate that they know each word. It is expected that not all the key words will be new words for each student, but this will be an important cooperative activity to get the unit underway.
(See the Learner's Guide for more information on how to use the activities.)

Within the activities, additional new vocabulary items will be encountered. Consequently, for the learner, the final list of new vocabulary in the semantic field of a basic human activity, shopping, will be significant.

Answers for some of the activities are available at www.ProLinguaAssociates.com. The answers along with the CD make *Shopping* an easy text for self-studiers.

Note that a number of characters appear throughout the units. A complete presentation will be found in Appendix 1. The characters' names are based on the sixteen phonemic vowels of English along with a few troublesome consonants. You can work on these pronunciation aspects explicitly or simply let them occur implicitly as you proceed through the text.

Appendix 1: Pronunciation
The Cast of Main Characters

Jean   Jill   Bert   Brooke   Hugh   Ruth

Jeff   Jane   Max   Chuck   Joy   Joe

Mike   Jon   Howie   Paul

Secondary Characters

Vern   Fern   Beth   Bess   Bev   Lou

Appendix 2: Money

Key Word Index

2% milk 4
affordable 9
aisle 1
antacid 7
apples 3
attendant 8
bag 1
bagels 5
bakery 1
banana 3
bargains 11
battery 10
beauty products 7
beef 2
beer 6
beets 3
bench 11
big box store 11
bolt 10
boots 8
bread 5
broom 10
brush 10
butter 4
cabbage 3
calamari 2
campfire wood 6
candy 6
carrots 3
car wash 8
cash 8
cashier 1
catfish 2
chain 7

challenge 11
to charge 8
cheapest 8
checkout 1
cheddar cheese 4
chicken 2
to choose 8
clam 12
closed 1
clothing 11
coat 9
cod 2
coffee 5
coleslaw 5
comfort 11
condition 9
conditioner 7
convenient 6
cookie 5
corn 3
crab 2
cream 4
credit 8
to cut 9
dairy 1
debit 8
deli 6
department 1
dietary supplements 7
domestic 5
drill 10
dustpan 10
electronics 11
employee 1

empty 8
entrance 1
exit 1
express 1
eyecare 7
to fit 9
flashlight 10
flounder 2
food court 11
foot care 7
frozen food 1
full-serve 8
furniture 9
gallon 4
gas cap 8
gas station 8
gas tank 8
gloves 9
glue 10
grade 8
grapefruit 3
grapes 3
grated cheese 4
ground beef 2
hair care 6
half and half 4
half-gallon 4
half-pint 4
hallway 11
hammer 10
hot dog 2
housewares 9
ice 6
ice cream 4

icing 5
imported 5
inexpensive 9
to insert 8
jacket 9
kiosk 11
lamb 2
laxative 7
lettuce 3
loaf 5
lottery ticket 7
magazine 5
manager 1
margarine 4
meat 1
melons 3
milk 1
mussels 2
nails 10
neighborhood 6
newspaper 6
nozzle 8
nut 10
one-hour photo 7
open 1
oranges 3
oven 5
pack 5
pain killer 6
paint 10
paintbrush 10
parking lot 11
pasta 5
pastry 5

peaches 3
pears 3
pharmacist 7
pharmacy 7
pie 5
pills 7
pint 4
pork 2
potato 3
poultry 2
prescription 7
produce 1
pump 8
to pump 8
to put in 8
quart 4
receipt 8
refill 7
to replace 8
to rest 11
restroom 6
road map 6
salmon 2
sandals 9
sandwich 6
sausage 2
saw 10
safe 11
scallops 2
seafood 2
screw 10
screw driver 10
shampoo 7
shellfish 2

shop 11
shopping bag 1
shopping basket 1
shopping cart 1
shorts 9
shrimp 2
sliced 5
snacks 6
socializing 11
soft drink 5
soup 6
spinach 3
strawberries 3
strollers 11
sweater 9
Swiss cheese 5
takeout 5
tape 10
tilapia 2
tomato 3
tools 10
tuna 2
turkey 2
to try on 9
turnover 5
vendor 11
vitamins 7
to watch 11
whole milk 4
wrench 10
yogurt 4

OTHER VOCABULARY DEVELOPMENT BOOKS

Money. The Vocabulary of the Financial World. Audio CD available.

The Zodiac. The Vocabulary of Human Qualities and Characteristics. Audio CD available.

American Holidays.* 20 units/holidays. 195 words exploring traditions, customs, and backgrounds of the holidays. Audio CD available.

Potluck. Exploring North American Meals, Culinary Practices, and Places. 24 Units. 288 key words. 2 audio CDs available.

Wheels and Wings. 143 key words associated with the world of transportation and travel.

OTHER BOOKS ON VOCABULARY

Lexicarry.* Pictures for Learning Languages. Over 4500 everyday words and expressions. Word lists in twelve languages correlated with the drawings.

Getting a Fix on Vocabulary. A student text that focuses on affixation. Includes all the common prefixes and suffixes and the most common bases. Text also includes "radio news" on audio CD.

The Learner's Lexicon. A word frequency list of 2400 words, divided into 300-, 600-, 1200-, and 2400-word lists.

Got It! Vocabulary games where teams compete to come up with words that are associated with lexical sets – work, food, body, weather, etc.

Go Fish. Seven beginning-level card games that focus on the basic vocabulary of the home (86 words).

Coloring in English. Beginning-level vocabulary-building coloring book for kids and adults. 40 pictures; 400 words.

A-Z Picture Activities.* Phonics and Vocabulary for Emerging Readers. One unit for each letter of the alphabet. Dozens of pictures. Audio CD available.

The Idiom Book.* 1001 Idioms in Two-Page Lessons. Based on everyday events. 2 audio CDs available.

A Phrasal Verb Affair.* 250 phrasal verbs from "add up to" to "zero in on" in a soap opera of 15 episodes. Audio CD available.

The ESL Miscellany: A Treasury of Cultural and Linguistic Information – 2020 Sixth Edition. There is a 13-page section on the Morphology and Lexicon of North American English and an 84-page section, The Communicative Aspect, consisting of 10 pages of vocabulary lists relating to situational contexts in which we use English and a further 63 pages of lists of topical vocabulary from food to technology. Other sections on The Linguistic Aspect, Communicative Functions, The Cultural Aspect, The Metalinguistic Aspect (including a list of 600 high-frequency words), and The Paralinguistic Aspect are deep sources of vocabulary in context. The Miscellany, 2015 Fifth Edition, * is available digitally.

*Available as eBook/digital editions

ProLinguaAssociates.com